TO:

_____

FROM:

_____

~~TEENS~~
30 DAILY DEVOTIONALS

INSTANT MESSAGES ~~FROM~~ GOD for guys

Simon & Schuster, Inc.

NEW YORK LONDON TORONTO SYDNEY

Simon & Schuster, Inc.

1230 Avenue of the Americas, New York, New York 10020

Scripture quotations are taken from:

Scriptures marked NIV® are from the *Holy Bible, New International Version®*. Copyright © 1973, 1978, 1984 by International Bible Society. Used by permission of Zondervan Publishing House. All rights reserved.

Scriptures marked NASB are taken from the *New American Standard Bible®*. Copyright © The Lockman Foundation 1960, 1962, 1963, 1968, 1971, 1972, 1973, 1975, 1977, 1995. Used by permission. (www.Lockman.org).

Scriptures marked NKJV are taken from the *New King James Version®*. Copyright © 1982 by Thomas Nelson, Inc. Used by permission. All rights reserved.

Scriptures marked NLT are taken from the *Holy Bible, New Living Translation*. Copyright © 1996. Used by permission of Tyndale House Publishers, Inc., Wheaton, Illinois 60189. All rights reserved.

Scriptures marked NCV are quoted from *The Holy Bible, New Century Version*. Copyright © 1987, 1988, 1991 by Word Publishing, Nashville, TN 37214. Used by permission.

Scriptures marked KJV are taken from the *King James Version*.

Scripture quotations marked MSG are taken from *The Message*. Copyright © by Eugene H. Peterson 1993, 1994, 1995. Used by permission of NavPress Publishing Group.

Scripture quotations marked ICB are taken from the *International Children's Bible, New Century Version*. Copyright © 1986, 1988 by Word Publishing, Nashville, TN 37214. Used by permission.

Scripture quotations marked TLB are taken from *The Living Bible*. Copyright © 1971. Used by permission of Tyndale House Publishers, Inc., Wheaton, Illinois 60189. All rights reserved.

Scripture quotations marked HCSB are taken from the *Holman Christian Standard Bible®*. Copyright © 1999, 2000, 2002, 2003 by Holman Bible Publishers. Used by permission. Holman Christian Standard Bible®, Holman CSB®, and HCSB® are federally registered trademarks of Holman Bible Publishers.

Cover Design by Kim Russell / Wahoo Designs
Page Layout by Bart Dawson

Manufactured in the United States of America

10 9 8 7 6 5 4 3 2 1

ISBN-13: 978-1-4169-1601-7
ISBN-10: 1-4169-1601-6

TEENS

30 DAILY DEVOTIONALS

INSTANT MESSAGES

FROM GOD

for guys

TABLE OF CONTENTS

INTRODUCTION

Everybody knows you're a very busy guy. But here's a question: can you squeeze at least five minutes each day into your hectic schedule—five minutes to spend with God? If you're a wise guy, the answer will be a resounding yes. Why? Because God is trying to get important messages through to you, that's why!

God has a plan for everything, and that includes you. But figuring out that plan may not be easy. That's why you need to talk to God . . . a lot. The more you talk to your Creator, the sooner He will help you figure out exactly what plans He has in store for you. So do yourself a favor: start talking to Him now. As you begin that conversation, this little book can help. This text contains 30 short devotional readings, messages from God that should be of particular interest to a busy guy like you.

Would you like to have a life that's above and beyond the ordinary? Talk to God about it. Do you have questions that you can't answer? God has answers. Are you seeking to improve some aspect of your life? The Bible is the greatest self-improvement book of all time. Do you want to be a better person and a better Christian? If so, ask for God's help and ask for it many times each day . . . starting with a regular, heartfelt morning devotional. Even five minutes is enough time to change your day . . . and your life.

Instant Message #1

RE:

GOD WANTS YOUR ATTENTION

Be still, and know that I am God.

Psalm 46:10 NKJV

Who is in charge of your heart? Is it God, or is it something else? Have you given Christ your heart, your soul, your talents, your time, and your testimony? Or are you giving Him little more than a few hours each Sunday morning?

In the book of Exodus, God warns that we should place no gods before Him. Yet all too often, we place our Lord in second, third, or fourth place as we worship other things. When we unwittingly place possessions or relationships above our love for the Creator, we create big problems for ourselves.

God wants your attention. Are you willing to give it? Make certain that the honest answer to this question is a resounding yes. In the life of every believer, God should come first. And that's precisely the place that He deserves in your heart.

In the long run there will be but two kinds of men: those who love God and those who love something else.

St. Augustine

MORE MESSAGES FROM GOD'S WORD

You will seek Me and find Me
when you search for Me
with all your heart.

Jeremiah 29:13 HCSB

You shall have no other gods before Me.

Exodus 20:3 NKJV

For it is written,
"You shall worship the Lord your God,
and Him only you shall serve."

Matthew 4:10 NKJV

Instant Tip:

Find the best time of the day to spend with God: Hudson Taylor, an English missionary, wrote, "Whatever is your best time in the day, give that to communion with God." That's powerful advice that leads to a powerful faith.

My Prayer to God:

Dear Lord, in the quiet moments of this day, I will turn my thoughts and prayers to You. In these silent moments, I will sense Your presence, and I will seek Your will for my life, knowing that when I accept Your peace, I will be blessed today and throughout eternity. Amen

Instant Message #2

RE:

GOD WANTS YOU TO SPEND A FEW MINUTES (AT LEAST!) WITH HIM EVERY DAY

Let the words of my mouth and the meditation of my heart be acceptable in Your sight, O Lord, my strength and my Redeemer.

Psalm 19:14 NKJV

Each day has 1,440 minutes—can you give God a few of them each morning? Of course you can . . . and of course your should!

Do you squeeze God into your busy schedule with an occasional prayer before meals (and maybe with a quick visit to church on Sunday)? Or do you please God by talking to Him far more often than that? If you're wise, you'll form the habit of spending time with God every day.

Has the busy pace of life here in the 21st century robbed you of time with God? If so, it's time to reorder your priorities and your life. Nothing is more important than the time you spend with your Heavenly Father, so slow down and have a word or two with Him. Then, claim the peace and abundance that can be yours when you regularly spend time with your Heavenly Father. His peace is offered freely; it has been paid for in full; it is yours for the asking. So ask. And then share.

Be still: pause and discover that God is God.

Charles Swindoll

MORE MESSAGES FROM GOD'S WORD

Morning by morning he wakens me and opens my understanding to his will. The Sovereign Lord has spoken to me, and I have listened.

Isaiah 50:4-5 NLT

It is good to give thanks to the Lord, to sing praises to the Most High. It is good to proclaim your unfailing love in the morning, your faithfulness in the evening.

Psalm 92:1-2 NLT

But grow in the grace and knowledge of our Lord and Savior Jesus Christ. To Him be the glory both now and to the day of eternity.

2 Peter 3:18 HCSB

Instant Tip:

Trust God's Timing. God has very big plans in store for your life, so trust Him and wait patiently for those plans to unfold. And remember: God's timing is best, so don't allow yourself to become discouraged if things don't work out exactly as you wish. Instead of worrying about your future, entrust it to God. He knows exactly what you need and exactly when you need it.

My Prayer to God:

Lord, Your Holy Word is a light unto the world; let me study it, trust it, and share it with all who cross my path. Let me discover You, Father, in the quiet moments of the day. And, in all that I say and do, help me to be a worthy witness as I share the Good News of Your perfect Son and Your perfect Word. Amen

Instant Message #3

RE:

GOD WANTS YOU TO BE PATIENT

Better a patient man than a warrior,
a man who controls his temper
than one who takes a city.

Proverbs 16:32 NIV

Are you a perfectly patient fellow? If so, feel free to skip the rest of this page. But if you're not, here's something to think about: If you really want to become a more patient person, God is ready and willing to help.

The Bible promises that when you sincerely seek God's help, He will give you the things that you need—and that includes patience. But God won't force you to become a more patient person. If you want to become a more mature Christian, you've got to do some of the work yourself—and the best time to start doing that work is now.

So, if you want to gain patience and maturity, bow your head and start praying about it. Then, rest assured that with God's help, you can most certainly make yourself a more patient, understanding, mature Christian.

God never hurries. There are no deadlines against which He must work. To know this is to quiet our spirits and relax our nerves.

A. W. Tozer

MORE MESSAGES FROM GOD'S WORD

Knowing God leads to self-control.
Self-control leads to patient endurance,
and patient endurance leads to godliness.

2 Peter 1:6 NLT

Patience and encouragement come from God.
And I pray that God will help you all agree
with each other the way Christ Jesus wants.

Romans 15:5 NCV

But if we look forward to something
we don't have yet, we must wait
patiently and confidently.

Romans 8:25 NLT

Instant Tip:

Waiting Faithfully for God's Plan To Unfold Is More Important Than Understanding God's Plan. Ruth Bell Graham once said, " When I am dealing with an all-powerful, all-knowing God, I, as a mere mortal, must offer my petitions not only with persistence, but also with patience. Someday I'll know why." Even when you can't understand God's plans, you must trust Him and never lose faith!

My Prayer to God:

Heavenly Father, let me wait quietly for You. Let me live according to Your plan and according to Your timetable. When I am hurried, slow me down. When I become impatient with others, give me empathy. Today, I want to be a patient Christian, Lord, as I trust in You and in Your master plan. Amen

Instant Message #4

RE:

YOU'VE GOT TALENTS— DISCOVER THEM

> *God has given gifts to each of you from his great variety of spiritual gifts. Manage them well so that God's generosity can flow through you.*
>
> 1 Peter 4:10 NLT

When God made you, he equipped you with an array of talents and abilities that are uniquely yours. It's up to you to discover those talents and to use them, but sometimes the world will encourage you to do otherwise. At times, our society will attempt to cubbyhole you, to standardize you, and to make you fit into a particular, preformed mold. Perhaps God has other plans.

Have you found something in this life that you're passionate about? Something that inspires you to jump out of bed in the morning and hit the ground running? And does your work honor the Creator by making His world a better place? If so, congratulations: you're using your gifts well.

Sometimes, because you're an imperfect human being, you may become so wrapped up in meeting society's expectations that you fail to focus on God's expectations. To do so is a mistake of major proportions—don't make it. Instead, seek God's guidance as you focus your energies on becoming the best "you" that you can possibly be.

What's the best way to thank God for the gifts that He has given you? By using them. And you might as well start using those gifts today.

MORE MESSAGES FROM GOD'S WORD

Do not neglect the gift that is in you.

1 Timothy 4:14 HCSB

I remind you to fan into flame the gift of God.

2 Timothy 1:6 NIV

There are different kinds of gifts,
but they are all from the same Spirit.
There are different ways to serve
but the same Lord to serve.

1 Corinthians 12:4–5 NCV

You are valuable just because you exist.
Not because of what you do or what you have
done, but simply because you are.

Max Lucado

Instant Tip:

Converting Talent Into Skill Requires Work:
Remember the old adage: "What we are is
God's gift to us; what we become is our gift to
God."

My Prayer to God:

*Lord, I have so much to learn and so
many ways to improve myself, but You
love me just as I am. Thank You for Your
love and for Your Son. And, help me to
become the person that You want me
to become. Amen*

Instant Message #5

RE:

NO MORE ANGRY OUTBURSTS, PLEASE!

*Everyone should be quick to listen,
slow to speak and slow to become angry,
for man's anger does not bring about
the righteous life that God desires.*

James 1:19-20 NIV

If you're like most guys, you know a thing or two about anger. After all, everybody gets mad occasionally, and you're probably no exception.

Anger is a natural human emotion that is sometimes necessary and appropriate. Even Jesus became angry when confronted with the moneychangers in the temple: "And Jesus entered the temple and drove out all those who were buying and selling in the temple, and overturned the tables of the moneychangers and the seats of those who were selling doves" (Matthew 21:12 NASB).

Righteous indignation is an appropriate response to evil, but God does not intend that anger should rule our lives. Far from it. God intends that we turn away from anger whenever possible and forgive our neighbors just as we seek forgiveness for ourselves.

Life is full of frustrations: some great and some small. On occasion, you, like Jesus, will confront evil, and when you do, you may respond as He did: vigorously and without reservation. But, more often your frustrations will be of the more mundane variety. As long as you live here on earth, you will face countless opportunities to lose your temper over small, relatively insignificant events: a traffic jam, an inconsiderate comment, or a broken promise. When you are tempted to lose your temper over the minor inconveniences of life, don't. Instead of turning up the heat, walk away. Turn away from anger, hatred, bitterness, and regret. Turn, instead, to God. When you do, you'll be following His commandments and giving yourself a priceless gift…the gift of peace.

WHEN YOU STRIKE OUT IN ANGER, YOU MAY MISS THE OTHER PERSON, BUT YOU WILL ALWAYS HIT YOURSELF.

Jim Gallery

Anger is the noise of the soul;
the unseen irritant of the heart;
the relentless invader of silence.

Max Lucado

When you get hot under the collar,
make sure your heart is prayer-conditioned.

Quips, Anonymous

Imagine your anger to be a kind of wild beast
. . . because it too has ferocious teeth
and claws, and if you don't tame it, it will
devastate all things . . . It not only hurts
the body; it even corrupts the health
of the soul, devouring, rending, tearing
to pieces all its strength, and making it
useless for everything.

St. John Chrysostom

MORE MESSAGES FROM GOD'S WORD

Don't become angry quickly, because getting angry is foolish.

Ecclesiastes 7:9 NCV

When you are angry, do not sin, and be sure to stop being angry before the end of the day. Do not give the devil a way to defeat you.

Ephesians 4:26–27 NCV

God's servant must not be argumentative, but a gentle listener and a teacher who keeps cool, working firmly but patiently with those who refuse to obey. You never know how or when God might sober them up with a change of heart and a turning to the truth.

2 Timothy 2:24-25 MSG

Instant Tip:

Count to ten . . . but don't stop there!: If you're angry with someone, don't say the first thing that comes to your mind. Instead, catch your breath and start counting until you are once again in control of your temper. If you count to a thousand and you're still counting, go to bed! You'll feel better in the morning.

My Prayer to God:

Lord, I can be so impatient, and I can become so angry. Calm me down, Lord, and give me the maturity and the wisdom to be a patient, forgiving Christian. Just as You have forgiven me, Father, let me forgive others so that I can follow the example of Your Son. Amen

Instant Message #6

RE:

WHEN TIMES GET TOUGH, KEEP THE FAITH

*The fundamental fact of existence is
that this trust in God, this faith,
is the firm foundation under everything
that makes life worth living.*

Hebrews 11:1 MSG

In the months and years ahead, your faith will be tested many times. Every life—including yours—is a series of successes and failures, celebrations and disappointments, joys and sorrows. Every step of the way, through every triumph and tragedy, God will stand by your side and strengthen you…if you have faith in Him. Jesus taught his disciples that if they had faith, they could move mountains. You can too.

If you place your faith, your trust, indeed your life in the hands of Christ Jesus, you'll be amazed at the marvelous things He can do with you and through you.

Today and every day, strengthen your faith through praise, through worship, through Bible study, and through prayer. God has big plans for you, so trust His plans and strengthen your faith in Him. With God, all things are possible, and He stands ready to help you accomplish miraculous things with your life…if you have faith.

**Faith means believing in advance
what will only make sense in reverse.**

Philip Yancey

MORE MESSAGES FROM GOD'S WORD

*We also have joy with our troubles, because
we know that these troubles produce patience.
And patience produces character,
and character produces hope.*

Romans 5:3-4 NCV

*Don't fret or worry. Instead of worrying, pray.
Let petitions and praises shape your worries
into prayers, letting God know your concerns.
Before you know it, a sense of God's wholeness,
everything coming together for good,
will come and settle you down. It's wonderful
what happens when Christ displaces
worry at the center of your life.*

Philippians 4:6-7 MSG

*The Lord lifts the burdens of those bent beneath
their loads. The Lord loves the righteous.*

Psalm 146:8 NLT

Instant Tip:

Faith Should Be Practiced More Than Studied. Vance Havner said, "Nothing is more disastrous than to study faith, analyze faith, make noble resolves of faith, but never actually to make the leap of faith." How true!

My Prayer to God:

Dear Lord, direct my path far from the temptations and distractions of this world, and make me a champion of the faith. Today I will honor You with my thoughts, my actions, and my prayers. I will worship You, Father, with thanksgiving in my heart and praise on my lips, this day and forever. Amen

Instant Message #7

RE:

IF YOU NEED STRENGTH, GOD CAN GIVE IT TO YOU

I am able to do all things through Him who strengthens me.

Philippians 4:13 HCSB

Where do you go to find strength? The gym? The health food store? The expresso bar? There's a better source of strength, of course, and that source is God. He is a never-ending source of strength and courage if you call upon Him.

Are you an energized Christian? You should be. But if you're not, you must seek strength and renewal from the source that will never fail: that source, of course, is your Heavenly Father. And rest assured—when you sincerely petition Him, He will give you all the strength you need to live victoriously for Him.

Have you "tapped in" to the power of God? Have you turned your life and your heart over to Him, or are you muddling along under your own power? The answer to this question will determine the quality of your life here on earth and the destiny of your life throughout all eternity. So start tapping in—and remember that when it comes to strength, God is the Ultimate Source.

MORE MESSAGES FROM GOD'S WORD

And He said to me, "My grace is sufficient for you, for My strength is made perfect in weakness."

2 Corinthians 12:9 NKJV

He gives strength to the weary and strengthens the powerless.

Isaiah 40:29 HCSB

Finally, be strengthened by the Lord and by His vast strength.

Ephesians 6:10 HCSB

God is great and God is powerful, but we must invite him to be powerful in our lives. His strength is always there, but it's up to us to provide a channel through which that power can flow.

Bill Hybels

Instant Tip:

Need Strength? Let God's Spirit Reign Over Your Heart. Anne Graham Lotz writes, "The amount of power you experience to live a victorious, triumphant Christian life is directly proportional to the freedom you give the Spirit to be Lord of your life!" And remember that the best time to begin living triumphantly is the present moment.

My Prayer to God:

Dear Lord, I will turn to You for strength. When my responsibilities seem overwhelming, I will trust You to give me courage and perspective. Today and every day, I will look to You as the ultimate source of my hope, my strength, my peace, and my salvation. Amen

Instant Message #8

RE:

IF YOU MAKE A MISTAKE, GOD WILL STAND BY YOU

If we confess our sins to him, he is faithful and just to forgive us and to cleanse us from every wrong.

1 John 1:9 NLT

If you've led a perfect life with absolutely no foul ups, blunders, mistakes, or flops, you can skip this chapter. But if you're like the rest of us, you know that occasional disappointments and failures are an inevitable part of life. These setbacks are simply the price of growing up and learning about life. But even when you experience bitter disappointments, you must never lose faith.

When times are tough, the Bible teaches us to persevere: "For you need endurance, so that after you have done God's will, you may receive what was promised." These reassuring words from Hebrews 10:36 (HCSB) remind us that when we persevere, we will eventually receive that which God has promised. Even when we fail, God is faithful. What's required of us is perseverance, not perfection.

When we encounter the inevitable difficulties of life here on earth, God stands ready to protect us. And, while we are waiting for God's plans to unfold, we can be comforted in the knowledge that our Creator can overcome any obstacle, even if we cannot.

MORE MESSAGES FROM GOD'S WORD

If you hide your sins, you will not succeed.
If you confess and reject them,
you will receive mercy.

Proverbs 28:13 NCV

If you listen to constructive criticism,
you will be at home among the wise.

Proverbs 15:31 NLT

I will instruct you and teach you in
the way you should go;
I will counsel you and watch over you.

Psalm 32:8 NIV

———————————————

No matter how badly we have failed,
we can always get up and begin again.
Our God is the God of new beginnings.

Warren Wiersbe

Instant Tip:

You can count on God's faithfulness in good times and bad. Max Lucado writes, "God's faithfulness has never depended on the faithfulness of his children. God is greater than our weakness. In fact, I think, it is our weakness that reveals how great God is." Enough said.

My Prayer to God:

Lord, sometimes I make mistakes and fall short of your commandments. When I do, forgive me, Father. And help me learn from my mistakes so that I can be a better servant to You and a better example to my friends and family. Amen

Instant Message #9

RE:

LIFE IS A MARATHON, NOT A SPRINT

Keep your eyes on Jesus, who both began
and finished this race we're in. Study how
he did it. Because he never lost sight of where
he was headed—that exhilarating finish
in and with God—he could put up with
anything along the way: cross, shame,
whatever. And now he's there, in the place
of honor, right alongside God.

Hebrews 12:2 MSG

A well-lived life is like a marathon, not a sprint—it calls for preparation, determination, and lots of perseverance. As an example of perfect perseverance, we Christians need look no further than our Savior, Jesus Christ.

Jesus finished what He began. Despite His suffering and despite the shame of the cross, Jesus was steadfast in His faithfulness to God. We, too, must remain faithful, especially during times of hardship. Sometimes, God may answer our prayers with silence, and when He does, we must patiently persevere.

Are you facing a difficult time in your life? If so, remember the words of Winston Churchill: "Never give in!" And remember this: whatever your problem, God can handle it. Your job is to keep persevering until He does.

Battles are won in the trenches, in the grit and grime of courageous determination; they are won day by day in the arena of life.

Charles Swindoll

MORE MESSAGES FROM GOD'S WORD

Patient endurance is what you need now,
so you will continue to do God's will.
Then you will receive all that he has promised.

Hebrews 10:36 NLT

Let us not become weary in doing good,
for at the proper time we will reap
a harvest if we do not give up.

Galatians 6:9 NIV

It is better to finish something than to start it.
It is better to be patient than to be proud.

Ecclesiastes 7:8 NCV

Instant Tip:

The World Encourages Instant Gratification but God's Work Takes Time. Remember the words of C. H. Spurgeon: "By perseverance, the snail reached the ark."

My Prayer to God:

Dear Lord, life is not a sprint, but a marathon. When the pace of my life becomes frantic, slow me down and give me perspective. Keep me steady and sure. When I become weary, let me persevere so that, in Your time, I might finish my work here on earth, and that You might then say, "Well done, my good and faithful servant." Amen

Instant Message #10

RE:

KINDNESS IS A CHOICE

> *Kind people do themselves a favor,*
> *but cruel people bring trouble*
> *on themselves.*
>
> Proverbs 11:17 NCV

If we believe the words of Proverbs 11:17—and we should—then we understand that kindness is its own reward. And, if we to obey the commandments of our Savior—and we should—we must sow seeds of kindness wherever we go.

Kindness is a choice. Sometimes, when we feel happy or generous, we find it easy to be kind. Other times, when we are discouraged or tired, we can scarcely summon the energy to utter a single kind word. But, God's commandment is clear: He intends that we make the conscious choice to treat others with kindness and respect, no matter our circumstances, no matter our emotions. Kindness, therefore, is a choice that we, as Christians must make many times each day.

Kindness, compassion, and forgiveness are hallmarks of your Christian faith. So today, in honor of the One who first showed compassion for you, it's your turn to teach your family and friends the art of kindness through your words and deeds. And then, you can open your arms wide to receive the gifts that God has in store for believers (like you) who are willing to obey His Holy Word.

MORE MESSAGES FROM GOD'S WORD

Be kind to each other, tenderhearted,
forgiving one another, just as God
through Christ has forgiven you.

Ephesians 4:32 NLT

Carry each other's burdens,
and in this way you will fulfill the law of Christ.

Galatians 6:2 NIV

Finally, all of you should be of one mind,
full of sympathy toward each other,
loving one another with tender hearts
and humble minds.

1 Peter 3:8 NLT

Instant Tip:

Kindness Every Day: Kindness should be part of our lives every day, not just on the days when we feel good. Don't try to be kind some of the time, and don't try to be kind to some of the people you know. Instead, try to be kind all of the time, and try to be kind to all the people you know. Remember, the Golden Rule starts with you!

My Prayer to God:

Lord, make me a loving, encouraging Christian. And, let my love for Christ be reflected through the kindness that I show to those who need the healing touch of the Master's hand. Amen

Instant Message #11

RE:

DON'T FALL IN LOVE WITH MONEY

> *For the love of money is a root of all sorts of evil, and some by longing for it have wandered away from the faith and pierced themselves with many griefs.*
>
> 1 Timothy 6:10 NASB

Are you a guy who's overly concerned with the stuff that money can buy? Hopefully not. On the grand stage of a well-lived life, material possessions should play a rather small role. Of course, we all need the basic necessities of life, but once we meet those needs for ourselves and for our families, the piling up of possessions creates more problems than it solves. Our real riches, of course, are not of this world. We are never really rich until we are rich in spirit.

Our society is in love with money and the things that money can buy. God is not. God cares about people, not possessions, and so must we. We must, to the best of our abilities, love our neighbors as ourselves, and we must, to the best of our abilities, resist the mighty temptation to place possessions ahead of people.

Money, in and of itself, is not evil; worshipping money is. So today, as you prioritize matters of importance in your life, remember that God is almighty, but the dollar is not.

**God is entitled to a portion of our income.
Not because he needs it,
but because we need to give it.**

James Dobson

MORE MESSAGES FROM GOD'S WORD

No one can serve two masters.
The person will hate one master and
love the other, or will follow one master
and refuse to follow the other.
You cannot serve both God and worldly riches.

Matthew 6:24 NCV

For the mind-set of the flesh is death,
but the mind-set of the Spirit is life and peace.

Romans 8:6 HCSB

Since we entered the world penniless
and will leave it penniless, if we have bread
on the table and shoes on our feet,
that's enough.

1 Timothy 6:7-8 MSG

Instant Tip:

Stuff 101: The world says, "Buy more stuff." God says, "Stuff isn't important." Believe God.

My Prayer to God:

Dear Lord, help make me a responsible steward of my financial resources. Let me trust Your Holy Word, and let me use my tithe for the support of Your church and for the eternal glory of Your Son. Amen

Instant Message #12

RE:

BE QUICK TO FORGIVE

Be gentle with one another, sensitive. Forgive one another as quickly and thoroughly as God in Christ forgave you.

Ephesians 4:32 MSG

Are you the kind of guy who carries a grudge? If so, you know sometimes it's very tough to forgive the people who have hurt you. And that's too bad because life would be much simpler if we could forgive people "once and for all" and be done with it. But forgiveness is seldom that easy. For most of us, the decision to forgive is straightforward, but the process of forgiving is more difficult. Forgiveness is a journey that requires effort, time, perseverance, and prayer.

Forgiveness is seldom easy, but it is always right. When we forgive those who have hurt us, we honor God by obeying His commandments. But when we harbor bitterness against others, we disobey God—with predictably unhappy results.

If there exists even one person whom you have not forgiven (and that includes yourself), follow God's commandment and His will for your life: forgive that person today. And remember that bitterness, anger, and regret are not part of God's plan for your life. Forgiveness is.

If you sincerely wish to forgive someone, pray for that person. And then pray for yourself by asking God to heal your heart. Don't expect forgiveness to be easy or quick, but rest assured: with God as your partner, you can forgive . . . and you will.

MORE MESSAGES FROM GOD'S WORD

Be even-tempered, content with second place, quick to forgive an offense. Forgive as quickly and completely as the Master forgave you. And regardless of what else you put on, wear love. It's your basic, all-purpose garment. Never be without it.

Colossians 3:13-14 MSG

*Hatred stirs up trouble,
but love forgives all wrongs.*

Proverbs 10:12 NCV

Our Father is kind; you be kind. Don't pick on people, jump on their failures, criticize their faults— unless, of course, you want the same treatment. Don't condemn those who are down; that hardness can boomerang. Be easy on people; you'll find life a lot easier.

Luke 6:36-37 MSG

Instant Tip:

Holding a grudge? Drop it. Never expect other people to be more forgiving than you are. And remember: the best time to forgive is now.

My Prayer to God:

Dear Lord, when I am bitter, You can change my unforgiving heart. And, when I am slow to forgive, Your Word reminds me that forgiveness is Your commandment. Let me be Your obedient servant, Lord, and let me forgive others just as You have forgiven me. Amen

Instant Message #13

RE:

INTEGRITY IS IMPORTANT

> *The man of integrity walks securely,*
> *but he who takes crooked paths*
> *will be found out.*
>
> Proverbs 10:9 NIV

You've heard the old saying so many times that you know it by heart: "Honesty is the best policy." But it's also worth noting that honesty isn't always the easiest policy. Sometimes, the truth hurts, and sometimes, it's tough to be a person of integrity . . . tough, but essential.

Charles Swindoll correctly observed, "Nothing speaks louder or more powerfully than a life of integrity." Godly men agree.

Integrity is a precious thing—difficult to build but easy to tear down. As believers in Christ, we must seek to live each day with discipline, honesty, and faith. When we do, integrity becomes a habit. And God smiles.

There's nothing like the power of integrity. It is a characteristic so radiant, so steady, so consistent, so beautiful, that it makes a permanent picture in our minds.

Franklin Graham

MORE MESSAGES FROM GOD'S WORD

Till I die, I will not deny my integrity. I will maintain my righteousness and never let go of it; my conscience will not reproach me as long as I live.

Job 27:5-6 NIV

May integrity and uprightness protect me, because my hope is in you.

Psalm 25:21 NIV

In everything set them an example by doing what is good. In your teaching show integrity, seriousness and soundness of speech that cannot be condemned, so that those who oppose you may be ashamed because they have nothing bad to say about us.

Titus 2:7 NIV

Instant Tip:

One of your greatest possessions is integrity . . . don't lose it. Billy Graham was right when he said: "Integrity is the glue that holds our way of life together. We must constantly strive to keep our integrity intact. When wealth is lost, nothing is lost; when health is lost, something is lost; when character is lost, all is lost."

My Prayer to God:

Lord, You are my Father in Heaven. You search my heart and know me far better than I know myself. May I be Your worthy servant, and may I live according to Your commandments. Let me be a person of integrity, Lord, and let my words and deeds be a testimony to You, today and always. Amen

Instant Message #14

RE:

WITH GOD ON YOUR SIDE, YOU'VE GOT NOTHING TO FEAR

Be strong and courageous. Do not be terrified; do not be discouraged, for the LORD your God will be with you wherever you go.

Joshua 1:9 NIV

Every human life (including yours) is a tapestry of events: some grand, some not-so-grand, and some downright disheartening. When we reach the mountaintops of life, praising God is easy. But, when the storm clouds form overhead and we find ourselves in the dark valley of despair, our faith is stretched, sometimes to the breaking point. As Christians, we can be comforted: Wherever we find ourselves, whether at the top of the mountain or the depths of the valley, God is there, and because He cares for us, we can live courageously.

Believing Christians have every reason to be courageous. After all, the ultimate battle has already been fought and won on the cross at Calvary. But, even dedicated followers of Christ may find their courage tested by the inevitable disappointments and tragedies that occur in the lives of believers and non-believers alike.

The next time you find your courage tested to the limit, remember that God is as near as your next breath, and remember that He offers salvation to His children. He is your shield and your strength; He is your protector and your deliverer. Call upon Him in your hour of need and then be comforted. Whatever your challenge, whatever your trouble, God can handle it.

MORE MESSAGES FROM GOD'S WORD

Finally, my brethren, be strong in the Lord
and in the power of His might.
Put on the whole armor of God,
that you may be able to stand against
the wiles of the devil.

Ephesians 6:10-11 NKJV

God is my shield, saving those
whose hearts are true and right.

Psalm 7:10 NLT

Those who trust the Lord are like Mount Zion,
which sits unmoved forever. As the mountains
surround Jerusalem, the Lord surrounds
his people now and forever.

Psalm 125:1-2 NCV

Instant Tip:

Jesus Is Looking for a Few Good Men . . . Like You. Charles Swindoll writes, "Our Lord is searching for people who will make a difference. Christians dare not dissolve into the background or blend into the neutral scenery of the world."

My Prayer to God:

Lord, sometimes I face challenges that leave me breathless. When I am fearful, let me lean upon You. Keep me ever mindful, Lord, that You are my God, my strength, and my shield. With You by my side, I have nothing to fear. And, with Your Son Jesus as my Savior, I have received the priceless gift of eternal life. Help me to be a grateful and courageous servant this day and every day. Amen

Instant Message #15

RE:

YOU'RE AN EXAMPLE ... BE A GOOD ONE

INSTANT MESSAGES

In every way be an example of doing good deeds. When you teach, do it with honesty and seriousness.

Titus 2:7 NCV

Whether we like it or not, all of us are examples. The question is not whether we will be examples to our families and friends; the question is simply what kind of examples will we be.

What kind of example are you? Are you the kind of person whose life serves as a powerful example of righteousness? Are you a young man whose behavior serves as a positive role model for younger folks? Are you the kind of guy whose actions, day in and day out, are honorable, ethical, and admirable? If so, you are not only blessed by God, but you are also a powerful force for good in a world that desperately needs positive influences such as yours.

D. L. Moody advised, "A man ought to live so that everybody knows he is a Christian, and most of all, his family ought to know." And that's sound advice because our families and friends are watching . . . and so, for that matter, is God.

We urgently need people who encourage and inspire us to move toward God and away from the world's enticing pleasures.

Jim Cymbala

MORE MESSAGES FROM GOD'S WORD

In everything you do, stay away from complaining and arguing, so that no one can speak a word of blame against you. You are to live clean, innocent lives as children of God in a dark world full of crooked and perverse people. Let your lives shine brightly before them.

Philippians 2:14-15 NLT

You are the light that gives light to the world. In the same way, you should be a light for other people. Live so that they will see the good things you do and will praise your Father in heaven.

Matthew 5:14,16 NCV

Do you want to be counted wise, to build a reputation for wisdom? Here's what you do: Live well, live wisely, live humbly. It's the way you live, not the way you talk, that counts.

James 3:13 MSG

Instant Tip:

Living Your Life and Shining Your Light . . . As a Christian, the most important light you shine is the light that your own life shines on the lives of others. May your light shine brightly, righteously, obediently, and eternally!

My Prayer to God:

Lord, make me a worthy example to my family and friends. And, let my words and my actions show people how my life has been changed by You. I will praise You, Father, by following in the footsteps of Your Son. Let others see Him through me. Amen

Instant Message #16

RE:

STRIVE FOR EXCELLENCE, NOT PERFECTION

Those who wait for perfect weather will never plant seeds; those who look at every cloud will never harvest crops. Plant early in the morning, and work until evening, because you don't know if this or that will succeed. They might both do well.

Ecclesiastes 11:4,6 NCV

So many expectations . . . so little time! As a guy living here in the 21st century, expectations can be very high indeed. The media delivers an endless stream of messages that tell you how to look, how to behave, how to dress, and what to drive. The media's expectations are impossible to meet—God's are not. God doesn't expect perfection . . . and neither should you.

If you find yourself bound up by the chains of perfectionism, it's time to ask yourself whom you're trying to impress, and why. If you're trying to impress other people, it's time to reconsider your priorities. Your first responsibility is to the Heavenly Father who created you and to His Son who saved you. Then, you bear a powerful responsibility to your family. But, when it comes to meeting society's unrealistic expectations, forget it!

Remember that when you accepted Christ as your Savior, God accepted you for all eternity. Now, it's your turn to accept yourself and your loved ones. When you do, you'll feel a tremendous weight being lifted from your shoulders. After all, pleasing God is simply a matter of obeying His commandments and accepting His Son. But as for pleasing everybody else? That's impossible!

MORE MESSAGES FROM GOD'S WORD

*Your beliefs about these things should be
kept secret between you and God.
People are happy if they can do what
they think is right without feeling guilty.*

Romans 14:22 NCV

*The fear of human opinion disables;
trusting in God protects you from that.*

Proverbs 29:25 MSG

*In thee, O Lord, do I put my trust;
let me never be put into confusion.*

Psalm 71:1 KJV

What makes a Christian a Christian is not
perfection but forgiveness.

Max Lucado

Instant Tip:

In This World, Strive for Excellence, Not Perfection. There will be plenty of time for perfection in the world to come.

My Prayer to God:

Dear Lord, you have taught us that love covers a multitude of shortcomings. Keep us mindful that perfection will be ours in the next world, not in this one. Help us to be accepting of our own imperfections, and give us the wisdom to accept—and even to cherish—the imperfections of those we love. Amen

Instant Message #17

RE:

IT'S A NEW DAY

The inward man is being renewed day by day.

2 Corinthians 4:16 NKJV

Even the most inspired Christian guys can find themselves running on empty. Even the most well-intentioned guys can run out of energy; even the most hopeful believers can be burdened by fears and doubts. And you are no exception.

When you're exhausted, or worried—or worse—there is a source from which you can draw the power needed to recharge your spiritual batteries. That source is God.

God intends that His children lead joyous lives filled with abundance and peace. But sometimes, abundance and peace seem very far away. During these difficult days, we must turn to God for renewal, and when we do, He will restore us.

Are you tired or troubled? Turn your heart toward God in prayer. Are you weak or worried? Take the time—or, more accurately, make the time—to delve deeply into God's Holy Word. Are you spiritually depleted? Call upon fellow believers to support you, and call upon Christ to renew your spirit and your life. When you do, you'll discover that the Creator of the universe stands always ready and always able to create a new sense of wonderment and joy in you.

MORE MESSAGES FROM GOD'S WORD

*The One who was sitting on the throne said,
"Look! I am making everything new!"
Then he said, "Write this, because these words
are true and can be trusted."*

Revelation 21:5 NCV

*When doubts filled my mind,
your comfort gave me renewed
hope and cheer.*

Psalm 94:19 NLT

*Create in me a pure heart, O God, and renew
a steadfast spirit within me. Do not cast me
from your presence or take your Holy Spirit
from me. Restore to me the joy of your salvation
and grant me a willing spirit, to sustain me.*

Psalm 51:10-12 NIV

Instant Tip:

Big, Bigger, and Very Big Plans. God has very big plans in store for your life, so trust Him and wait patiently for those plans to unfold. And remember: God's timing is best.

My Prayer to God:

Heavenly Father, sometimes I am troubled, and sometimes I grow weary. When I am weak, Lord, give me strength. When I am discouraged, renew me. When I am fearful, let me feel Your healing touch. Let me always trust in Your promises, Lord, and let me draw strength from those promises and from Your unending love. Amen

Instant Message #18

RE:

YOU'VE GOT PROBLEMS... AND GOD HAS SOLUTIONS

INSTANT MESSAGES

People who do what is right may have many problems, but the Lord will solve them all.

Psalm 34:19 NCV

Life is an adventure in problem-solving. The question is not whether we will encounter problems; the real question is how we will choose to address them. When it comes to solving the problems of everyday living, we often know precisely what needs to be done, but we may be slow in doing it—especially if what needs to be done is difficult. So we put off till tomorrow what should be done today.

As a young man living here in the 21st century, you have your own set of challenges. As you face those challenges, you may be comforted by this fact: Trouble, of every kind, is temporary. Yet God's grace is eternal. And worries, of every kind, are temporary. But God's love is everlasting. The troubles that concern you will pass. God remains. And for every problem, God has a solution.

The words of Psalm 34 remind us that the Lord solves problems for "people who do what is right." And usually, doing "what is right" means doing the uncomfortable work of confronting our problems sooner rather than later. So with no further ado, let the problem-solving begin . . . right now.

MORE MESSAGES FROM GOD'S WORD

Be joyful because you have hope. Be patient when trouble comes, and pray at all times.

Romans 12:12 NCV

I have told you these things, so that in me you may have peace. In this world you will have trouble. But take heart! I have overcome the world.

John 16:33 NIV

When troubles come and all these awful things happen to you, in future days you will come back to God, your God, and listen obediently to what he says. God, your God, is above all a compassionate God. In the end he will not abandon you, he won't bring you to ruin, he won't forget the covenant with your ancestors which he swore to them.

Deuteronomy 4:30-31 MSG

Instant Tip:

If It Wasn't for Trouble . . . we might think
we could handle our lives by ourselves. Jim
Cymbala writes, "Trouble is one of God's great
servants because it reminds us how much we
continually need the Lord." We should thank
the Lord for challenges that bring us closer to
Him.

My Prayer to God:

Lord, sometimes my problems are simply too big for me, but they are never too big for You. Let me turn my troubles over to You, Lord, and let me trust in You today and for all eternity. Amen

Instant Message #19

RE:

TODAY IS A GIFT ... USE IT

> *While it is daytime, we must continue doing the work of the One who sent me. Night is coming, when no one can work.*
>
> John 9:4 NCV

The words of John 9:4 remind us that "night is coming" for all of us. But until then, God gives us each day and fills it to the brim with possibilities. The day is presented to us fresh and clean at midnight, free of charge, but we must beware: Today is a non-renewable resource—once it's gone, it's gone forever. Our responsibility, of course, is to use this day in the service of God's will and in accordance with His commandments.

Today is a priceless gift that has been given to you by God—don't waste it. Don't stand on the sidelines as life's parade passes you by. Instead, search for the hidden possibilities that God has placed along your path. This day is a one-of-a-kind treasure that can be put to good use—or not. You challenge is to use this day joyfully and productively. And while you're at it, encourage others to do likewise. After all, night is coming when no one can work . . . .

Wherever you are, be all there.
Live to the hilt every situation
you believe to be the will of God.

Jim Elliot

MORE MESSAGES FROM GOD'S WORD

Since everything here today might well be gone tomorrow, do you see how essential it is to live a holy life?

2 Peter 3:11 MSG

Give thanks to the Lord, for He is good; His faithful love endures forever.

Psalm 106:1 HCSB

You will show me the way of life, granting me the joy of your presence and the pleasures of living with you forever.

Psalm 16:11 NLT

Instant Tip:

This is the Day: Remember the beautiful words found in the 118th Psalm: "This is the day which the LORD has made; let us rejoice and be glad in it" (v. 24). The present moment is a priceless gift. Treasure it; savor it; and use it.

My Prayer to God:

Help me, Father, to learn from the past but not live in it. And, help me to plan for the future but not to worry about it. This is the day that You have given me, Lord. Let me use it according to Your master plan, and let me give thanks for Your blessings. Enable me to live each moment to the fullest, totally involved in Your will. Amen

Instant Message #20

RE:

YOU CAN DEPEND ON GOD'S PROMISES

*Let us hold on to the confession of
our hope without wavering,
for He who promised is faithful.*

Hebrews 10:23 HCSB

Christianity is based upon promises that are contained in a unique book. That book is the Holy Bible. The Bible is a roadmap for life here on earth and for life eternal. As Christians, we are called upon to study its meaning, to trust its promises, to follow its commandments, and to share its Good News.

As believers, we should study the Bible each day and meditate upon its meaning for our lives. Otherwise, we deprive ourselves of a priceless gift from our Creator. God's Holy Word is, indeed, a transforming, life-changing, one-of-a-kind treasure. And, a passing acquaintance with the Good Book is insufficient for Christians who seek to obey God's Word and understand His will.

God has made promises to you, and He intends to keep them. So take God at His word: trust His promises and share them with your family, with your friends, and with the world.

We honor God by asking for great things when they are a part of His promise. We dishonor Him and cheat ourselves when we ask for molehills where He has promised mountains.

Vance Havner

MORE MESSAGES FROM GOD'S WORD

Heaven and earth will pass away,
but My words will never pass away.

Matthew 24:35 HCSB

But the word of the Lord endures forever.
And this is the word that was preached
as the gospel to you.

1 Peter 1:25 HCSB

For the word of God is living and effective
and sharper than any two-edged sword,
penetrating as far as to divide soul, spirit,
joints, and marrow; it is a judge of the ideas
and thoughts of the heart.

Hebrews 4:12 HCSB

Instant Tip:

Trust God's Word: Charles Swindoll writes, "There are four words I wish we would never forget, and they are, 'God keeps his word.'" And remember: When it comes to studying God's Word, school is always in session.

My Prayer to God:

Dear God, the Bible contains many promises. Let me trust Your promises, and let me live according to Your Holy Word, not just for today, but forever. Amen

Instant Message #21

RE:

TEMPTATION IS EVERYWHERE . . . AVOID IT!

*Let us throw off everything that hinders
and the sin that so easily entangles,
and let us run with perseverance
the race marked out for us.*

Hebrews 12:1 NIV

How hard is it to bump into temptation in this crazy world? Not very hard. The devil, it seems, is out on the street, working 24/7, causing pain and heartache in more ways than ever before. We, as Christians, must remain vigilant. Not only must we resist Satan when he confronts us, but we must also avoid those places where Satan can most easily tempt us. And, if we are to avoid the unending temptations of this world, we must arm ourselves with the Word of God.

In a letter to believers, Peter offers a stern warning: "Your adversary, the devil, prowls around like a roaring lion, seeking someone to devour" (I Peter 5:8 NASB). What was true in New Testament times is equally true in our own. Satan tempts his prey and then devours them (and it's up to you—and only you—to make sure that you're not one of the ones being devoured!).

As believing Christians, we must beware because temptations are everywhere. Satan is determined to win; we must be equally determined that he does not.

It is easier to stay out of temptation than to get out of it.

Rick Warren

MORE MESSAGES FROM GOD'S WORD

But remember that the temptations that come into your life are no different from what others experience. And God is faithful. He will keep the temptation from becoming so strong that you can't stand up against it. When you are tempted, he will show you a way out so that you will not give in to it.

1 Corinthians 10:13 NLT

Put on the full armor of God so that you can stand against the tactics of the Devil.

Ephesians 6:11 HCSB

Be sober! Be on the alert! Your adversary the Devil is prowling around like a roaring lion, looking for anyone he can devour.

1 Peter 5:8 HCSB

Instant Tip:

We Live in a Temptation Generation: You can find temptation in lots of places. Your job is to avoid those places!

My Prayer to God:

Dear Lord, I am an imperfect human being. When I have sinned, let me repent from my wrongdoings, and let me seek forgiveness—first from You, then from others, and finally from myself. Amen

Instant Message #22

RE:

CHRIST LOVES YOU

Do you think anyone is going to be able to drive a wedge between us and Christ's love for us? There is no way! Not trouble, not hard times, not hatred, not hunger, not homelessness, not bullying threats, not backstabbing, not even the worst sins listed in Scripture...I'm absolutely convinced that nothing, nothing living or dead, angelic or demonic, today or tomorrow, high or low, thinkable or unthinkable, absolutely nothing can get between us and God's love because of the way that Jesus our Master has embraced us.

Romans 8:35,38-39 MSG

How much does Christ love us? More than we, as mere mortals, can comprehend. His love is perfect and steadfast. Even though we are fallible and wayward, the Good Shepherd cares for us still. Even though we have fallen far short of the Father's commandments, Christ loves us with a power and depth that are beyond our understanding. The sacrifice that Jesus made upon the cross was made for each of us, and His love endures to the edge of eternity and beyond.

Christ's love changes everything. When you accept His gift of grace, you are transformed, not only for today, but also for all eternity. If you haven't already done so, accept Jesus Christ as Your Savior. He's waiting patiently for you to invite Him into your heart. Please don't make Him wait a single minute longer.

**He loved us not because we're lovable,
but because He is love.**

C. S. Lewis

MORE MESSAGES FROM GOD'S WORD

I am the good shepherd.
The good shepherd lays down his life
for the sheep.

John 10:11 HCSB

And remember, I am with you always,
to the end of the age.

Matthew 28:20 HCSB

Just as the Father has loved Me,
I also have loved you. Remain in My love.

John 15:9 HCSB

Instant Tip:

Jesus Loves Me, This I Know . . . But How Much? Here's how much: Jesus loves you so much that He gave His life so that you might live forever with Him in heaven. And how can you repay Christ's love? By accepting Him into your heart and by obeying His rules. When you do, He will love you and bless you today, tomorrow, and forever.

My Prayer to God:

Dear Lord, I offer thanksgiving and praise for the gift of Your only begotten Son. His love is boundless, infinite, and eternal. And, as an expression of my love for Him, let me share His message with my family, with my friends, and with the world. Amen

Instant Message #23

RE:

GOD HEARS YOUR PRAYERS

"'Relax, Daniel,' he continued, 'don't be afraid. From the moment you decided to humble yourself to receive understanding, your prayer was heard, and I set out to come to you.'"

Daniel 10:12 MSG

Are you a prayer warrior or have you retreated from God's battlefield? Do you pray about almost everything or about almost nothing? Do you pray only at mealtimes, or do you pray at all times? The answer to these questions will determine, to a surprising extent, the degree to which God will use you for the glory of His kingdom.

Jesus made it clear to His disciples: they should pray always. And so should we. Genuine, heartfelt prayer changes things, and it changes us. When we lift our hearts to our Father in heaven, we open ourselves to a never-ending source of divine wisdom and infinite love.

Your prayers are powerful, so pray. And as you go about your daily activities, remember God's instructions: "Rejoice always! Pray constantly. Give thanks in everything, for this is God's will for you in Christ Jesus" (1 Thessalonians 5:16-18 HCSB). Start praying in the morning and keep praying until you fall off to sleep at night. And rest assured: God is always listening, and He always wants to hear from you.

Next to the wonder of seeing my Savior will be, I think, the wonder that I made so little use of the power of prayer.

D. L. Moody

MORE MESSAGES FROM GOD'S WORD

If you don't know what you're doing, pray to the Father. He loves to help. You'll get his help, and won't be condescended to when you ask for it. Ask boldly, believingly, without a second thought. People who "worry their prayers" are like wind-whipped waves. Don't think you're going to get anything from the Master that way, adrift at sea, keeping all your options open.

James 1:5-8 MSG

I want men everywhere to lift up holy hands in prayer, without anger or disputing.

1 Timothy 2:8 NIV

Rejoice always! Pray constantly. Give thanks in everything, for this is God's will for you in Christ Jesus.

1 Thessalonians 5:16-18 HCSB

Instant Tip:

Sometimes, the answer is "No." God doesn't grant all of our requests, nor should He. We must understand that our prayers are answered by a sovereign, all-knowing God, and that we must trust His answers, whether the answer is "Yes," "No," or "Not Yet."

My Prayer to God:

Dear Lord, let me raise my hopes and my dreams, my worries and my fears to You. Let me be a worthy example to family and friends, showing them the importance and the power of prayer. Let me take everything to You in prayer, Lord, and when I do, let me trust in Your answers. Amen

RE:

GOD WANTS YOU TO LIVE ON PURPOSE, NOT BY ACCIDENT

God chose you to be his people, so I urge you now to live the life to which God called you.

Ephesians 4:1 NCV

"**W**hat did God put me here to do?" If you're like most guys, you've asked yourself that question on many occasions. Perhaps you have pondered over your future, uncertain of your plans or your next step. But even if you don't have a clear plan for the next step of your life's journey, you may rest assured that God does.

God has a plan for the universe, and He has a plan for you. He understands that plan as thoroughly and completely as He knows you. If you seek God's will earnestly and prayerfully, He will make His plans known to you in His own time and in His own way.

Do you sincerely seek to discover God's purpose for your life? If so, you must first be willing to live in accordance with His commandments. You must also study God's Word and be watchful for His signs. Finally, you should open yourself up to the Creator every day— beginning with this one—and you must have faith that He will soon reveal His plans to you.

Sometimes, God's plans and purposes may seem unmistakably clear to you. If so, push ahead. But other times, He may lead you through the wilderness before He directs you to the Promised Land. So be patient and keep seeking His will for your life. When you do, you'll be amazed at the marvelous things that an all-powerful, all-knowing God can do.

MORE MESSAGES FROM GOD'S WORD

Whatever you do, do all to the glory of God.

1 Corinthians 10:31 NKJV

You're sons of Light, daughters of Day.
We live under wide open skies
and know where we stand.
So let's not sleepwalk through life . . . .

1 Thessalonians 5:5-6 MSG

There is one thing I always do.
Forgetting the past and straining toward
what is ahead, I keep trying to reach
the goal and get the prize for which
God called me . . . .

Philippians 3:13–14 NCV

Instant Tip:

Discovering God's Purpose for Your Life Is Continuing Education. God's plan is unfolding day by day. If you keep your eyes and your heart open, He'll reveal His plans. God has big things in store for you, but He may have quite a few lessons to teach you before you are fully prepared to do His will and fulfill His purposes.

My Prayer to God:

Dear Lord, I seek to live a meaningful life; I will turn to You to find that meaning. I will study Your Word, I will obey Your commandments, I will trust Your providence, and I will honor Your Son. Give me Your blessings, Father, and lead me along a path that is pleasing to You, today, tomorrow, and forever. Amen

Instant Message #25

RE:

GOD WANTS YOU TO BECOME A MORE MATURE PERSON

*Grow in grace and understanding of
our Master and Savior, Jesus Christ.
Glory to the Master, now and forever! Yes!*

2 Peter 3:18 MSG

Are you about as mature as you're ever going to be? Hopefully not! When it comes to your faith, God doesn't intend for you to become "fully grown," at least not in this lifetime.

As a Christian man, you should continue to grow in the love and the knowledge of your Savior as long as you live. How? By studying God's Word, by obeying His commandments, and by allowing His Son to reign over your heart.

Are you seeking to become a more mature believer? Hopefully so, because that's exactly what God want's you to become . . . and it's exactly what your should want to become, too!

Salvation is not an event; it is a process.

Henry Blackaby

MORE MESSAGES FROM GOD'S WORD

When I was a child, I spoke and thought and reasoned as a child does. But when I grew up, I put away childish things.

1 Corinthians 13:11 NLT

Consider it pure joy, my brothers, whenever you face trials of many kinds, because you know that the testing of your faith develops perseverance. Perseverance must finish its work so that you may be mature and complete, not lacking anything.

James 1:2-4 NIV

Therefore let us leave the elementary teachings about Christ and go on to maturity....

Hebrews 6:1 NIV

Instant Tip:

Obedience Leads to Spiritual Growth: Oswald Sanders correctly observed, "We grow spiritually as our Lord grew physically: by a life of simple, unobtrusive obedience."

My Prayer to God:

Lord, help me to keep growing spiritually and emotionally. Let me live according to Your Word, and let me grow in my faith every day that I live. Amen

Instant Message #26

RE:

YOU HAVE PARTICULAR GIFTS THAT GOD WANTS YOU TO USE

INSTANT MESSAGES

Each man has his own gift from God;
one has this gift, another has that.

1 Corinthians 7:7 NIV

Face it: you've got an array of talents that need to be refined. All people possess special gifts—bestowed from the Father above—and you are no exception. But, your particular gift is no guarantee of success; it must be cultivated—by you—or it will go unused . . . and God's gift to you will be squandered.

Are you willing to do the hard work that's required to discover your talents and to develop them? If you are wise, you'll answer "yes." After all, if you don't make the most of your talents, who has the most to lose? You do!

So make a promise to yourself that you will earnestly seek to discover the talents that God has given you. Then, nourish those talents and make them grow. Finally, vow to share your gifts with the world for as long as God gives you the power to do so. After all, the best way to say "Thank You" for God's gifts is to use them.

God is still in the process of dispensing gifts, and He uses ordinary individuals like us to develop those gifts in other people.

Howard Hendricks

MORE MESSAGES FROM GOD'S WORD

God has given gifts to each of you from his great variety of spiritual gifts. Manage them well so that God's generosity can flow through you.

1 Peter 4:10 NLT

Now there are varieties of gifts, but the same Spirit. And there are varieties of ministries, and the same Lord.

1 Corinthians 12:4-5 NASB

Do not neglect the spiritual gift that is within you . . . .

1 Timothy 4:14 NASB

Instant Tip:

One Career or Many? Only a generation ago, men and women entered the workplace with the expectation that one career might last a lifetime. For most of us, those days are gone, probably forever. So keep learning, and keep your eyes open for the next big thing . . . it's probably just around the corner.

My Prayer to God:

Lord, I praise You for Your priceless gifts. I give thanks for Your creation, for Your Son, and for the unique talents and opportunities that You have given me. Let me use my gifts for the glory of Your kingdom, this day and every day. Amen

RE:

THE TIME TO ACCEPT GOD'S GRACE IS NOW

For if, by the trespass of the one man, death reigned through that one man, how much more will those who receive God's abundant provision of grace and of the gift of righteousness reign in life through the one man, Jesus Christ.

Romans 5:17 NIV

Here's the great news: God's grace is not earned . . . and thank goodness it's not! If God's grace were some sort of reward for good behavior, none of us could earn enough Brownie Points to win the big prize. But it doesn't work that way. Grace is a free offer from God. By accepting that offer, we transform our lives today and forever.

God's grace is not just any old gift; it's the ultimate gift, and we owe Him our eternal gratitude. Our Heavenly Father is waiting patiently for each of us to accept His Son and receive His grace. Let us accept that gift today so that we might enjoy God's presence now and throughout all eternity.

God's grace is indeed a gift from the heart—God's heart. And as believers, we must accept God's precious gift thankfully, humbly, and, immediately—today is never too soon because tomorrow may indeed be too late.

Christ is no Moses, no exactor, no giver of laws, but a giver of grace, a Savior; he is infinite mercy and goodness, freely and bountifully given to us.

Martin Luther

MORE MESSAGES FROM GOD'S WORD

My grace is sufficient for you,
for My strength is made perfect in weakness.

2 Corinthians 12:9 NKJV

For by grace you are saved through faith,
and this is not from yourselves; it is God's gift—
not from works, so that no one can boast.

Ephesians 2:8-9 HCSB

And we have seen and testify that the Father
has sent the Son as Savior of the world.

1 John 4:14 NKJV

Instant Tip:

God's Grace Is Always Available: Jim Cymbala writes, " No one is beyond his grace. No situation, anywhere on earth, is too hard for God." If you sincerely seek God's grace, He will give it freely. So ask, and you will receive.

My Prayer to God:

Lord, Your grace is a gift that cannot be earned. It is a gift that was given freely when I accepted Your Son as my personal Savior. Freely have I received Your gifts, Father. Let me freely share my gifts, my possessions, my time, my energy, and my faith. And let my words, my thoughts, my prayers, and my deeds bring honor to You and to Your Son, now and forever. Amen

Instant Message #28

RE:

GOD DESERVES YOUR PRAISE

From the rising of the sun to its setting,
the name of the LORD is to be praised.

Psalm 113:3 NASB

When is the best time to praise God? In church? Before dinner is served? When we tuck little children into bed? None of the above. The best time to praise God is all day, every day, to the greatest extent we can, with thanksgiving in our hearts, and with a song on our lips.

Too many of us, even well-intentioned believers, tend to "compartmentalize" our waking hours into a few familiar categories: work, rest, play, family time, and worship. To do so is a mistake. Worship and praise should be woven into the fabric of everything we do; it should never be relegated to a weekly three-hour visit to church on Sunday morning.

Theologian Wayne Oates once admitted, "Many of my prayers are made with my eyes open. You see, it seems I'm always praying about something, and it's not always convenient—or safe—to close my eyes." Dr. Oates understood that God always hears our prayers and that the relative position of our eyelids is of no concern to Him.

Today, find a little more time to lift your concerns to God in prayer, and praise Him for all that He has done. Whether your eyes are open or closed, He's listening.

MORE MESSAGES FROM GOD'S WORD

I will praise You with my whole heart.

Psalm 138:1 NKJV

Is anyone happy? Let him sing songs of praise.

James 5:13 NIV

*Through Him then, let us continually offer up
a sacrifice of praise to God, that is,
the fruit of lips that give thanks to His name.*

Hebrews 13:15 NASB

Praise—lifting up our heart and hands,
exulting with our voices, singing his praises—
is the occupation of those who dwell
in the kingdom.

Max Lucado

Instant Tip:

Praise Him! One of the main reasons you go to church is to praise God. But, you need not wait until Sunday rolls around to thank your Heavenly Father. Instead, you can praise Him many times each day by saying silent prayers that only He can hear.

My Prayer to God:

Dear Lord, I will praise You today and every day that I live. And, I will praise Your Son, the Savior of my life. Christ's love is boundless and eternal. Let my thoughts, my prayers, my words, and my deeds praise Him now and forever. Amen

Instant Message #29

RE:

GOD WANTS YOU TO BE THANKFUL

Enter his gates with thanksgiving,
go into his courts with praise.
Give thanks to him and bless his name.

Psalm 100:4 NLT

Are you basically a thankful guy? Do you appreciate the stuff you've got and the life that you're privileged to live? You most certainly should be thankful. After all, when you stop to think about it, God has given you more blessings than you can count. So the question of the day is this: will you slow down long enough to thank your Heavenly Father . . . or not?

Sometimes, life here on earth can be complicated, demanding, and frustrating. When the demands of life leave you rushing from place to place with scarcely a moment to spare, you may fail to pause and thank your Creator for the countless blessings He has given you. Failing to thank God is understandable . . . but it's wrong.

God's Word makes it clear: a wise heart is a thankful heart. Period. You Heavenly Father has blessed you beyond measure, and you owe Him everything, including your thanks. God is always listening—are you willing to say thanks? It's up to you, and the next move is yours.

The heathen misrepresent God by worshipping idols; we misrepresent God by our murmuring and our complaining.

C. H. Spurgeon

MORE MESSAGES FROM GOD'S WORD

Thanks be to God for His indescribable gift!

2 Corinthians 9:15 NKJV

Give thanks in all circumstances;
for this is God's will for you in Christ Jesus.

1 Thessalonians 5:18 NIV

I will thank you, Lord, with all my heart;
I will tell of all the marvelous things you have
done. I will be filled with joy because of you.
I will sing praises to your name, O Most High.

Psalm 9:1-2 NLT

Instant Tip:

When Is the Best Time to Say "Thanks" to God? Any Time. God loves you all the time, and that's exactly why you should praise Him all the time.

My Prayer to God:

Dear Lord, sometimes, amid the demands of the day, I lose perspective, and I fail to give thanks for Your blessings and for Your love. Today, help me to count those blessings, and let me give thanks to You, Father, for Your love, for Your grace, for Your blessings, and for Your Son. Amen

Instant Message #30

RE:

GOD WANTS YOU TO SERVE OTHERS

> *But he who is greatest among you shall be your servant.*
>
> Matthew 23:11 NKJV

The words of Jesus are clear: the most esteemed men and women in this world are not the big shots who jump up on stage and hog the spotlight; the greatest among us are those who are willing to become humble servants.

Are you willing to become a servant for Christ? Are you willing to pitch in and make the world a better place, or are you determined to keep all your blessings to yourself. Hopefully, you are determined to follow Christ's example by making yourself an unselfish servant to those who need your help.

Today, you may be tempted to take more than you give. But if you feel the urge to be selfish, resist that urge with all your might. Don't be stingy, selfish, or self-absorbed. Instead, serve your friends quietly and without fanfare. Find a need and fill it . . . humbly. Lend a helping hand…anonymously. Share a word of kindness . . . with quiet sincerity. As you go about your daily activities, remember that the Savior of all humanity made Himself a servant, and we, as His followers, must do no less.

MORE MESSAGES FROM GOD'S WORD

There are different kinds of gifts,
but they are all from the same Spirit.
There are different ways to serve
but the same Lord to serve.

1 Corinthians 12:4–5 NCV

Therefore, since we receive a kingdom which
cannot be shaken, let us show gratitude,
by which we may offer to God an acceptable
service with reverence and awe . . . .

Hebrews 12:28 NASB

If they serve Him obediently,
they will end their days in prosperity
and their years in happiness.

Job 36:11 HCSB

Instant Tip:

Talk is cheap. Real ministry has legs. When it comes to serving others, make sure that you back up your words with deeds.

My Prayer to God:

Lord, make me a loving, encouraging, compassionate Christian. And, let my love for Christ be reflected through the kindness that I show to my family, to my friends, and to all who need the healing touch of the Master's hand. Amen

RE:

BIBLE VERSES TO CONSIDER

ATTITUDE

There is one thing I always do.
Forgetting the past and straining toward what
is ahead, I keep trying to reach the goal and
get the prize for which God called me . . . .

Philippians 3:13–14 NCV

For God has not given us a spirit of fear,
but of power and of love and of a sound mind.

2 Timothy 1:7 NLT

Keep your eyes focused on what is right,
and look straight ahead to what is good.

Proverbs 4:25 NCV

You were taught, with regard to your former
way of life, to put off your old self, which is being
corrupted by its deceitful desires; to be made
new in the attitude of your minds; and to put
on the new self, created to be like God in true
righteousness and holiness.

Ephesians 4:22-24 NIV

A miserable heart means a miserable life; a cheerful heart fills the day with a song.

Proverbs 15:15 MSG

COURAGE

Be strong and courageous, and do the work.
Don't be afraid or discouraged,
for the Lord God, my God, is with you.
He won't leave you or forsake you.

1 Chronicles 28:20 HCSB

For God has not given us a spirit of fearfulness,
but one of power, love, and sound judgment.

2 Timothy 1:7 HCSB

Haven't I commanded you: be strong and
courageous? Do not be afraid or discouraged,
for the Lord your God is with you
wherever you go.

Joshua 1:9 HCSB

But when Jesus heard it, He answered him,
"Don't be afraid. Only believe."

Luke 8:50 HCSB

Be alert, stand firm in the faith, be brave and strong.

1 Corinthians 16:13 HCSB

GOD'S LOVE

For God loved the world in this way:
He gave His only Son, so that everyone
who believes in Him will not perish
but have eternal life.

John 3:16 HCSB

For the Lord is good, and His love is eternal;
His faithfulness endures through
all generations.

Psalm 100:5 HCSB

[Because of] the Lord's faithful love we do not
perish, for His mercies never end. They are new
every morning; great is Your faithfulness!

Lamentations 3:22-23 HCSB

Whoever is wise will observe these things,
and they will understand the
lovingkindness of the Lord.

Psalm 107:43 NKJV

Help me, Lord my God; save me according to Your faithful love.

Psalm 109:26 HCSB

HAPPINESS

I've learned by now to be quite content whatever my circumstances. I'm just as happy with little as with much, with much as with little. I've found the recipe for being happy whether full or hungry, hands full or hands empty.

Philippians 4:11-12 MSG

I will praise you, Lord, with all my heart. I will tell all the miracles you have done. I will be happy because of you; God Most High, I will sing praises to your name.

Psalms 9:1-2 NCV

How happy are those who can live in your house, always singing your praises. How happy are those who are strong in the Lord . . . .

Psalm 84:4-5 NLT

A happy heart makes the face cheerful, but heartache crushes the spirit.

Proverbs 15:13 NIV

A cheerful heart is good medicine.

Proverbs 17:22 NIV

CHANGE

*John said, "Change your hearts and lives
because the kingdom of heaven is near."*

Matthew 3:2 NCV

*Therefore do not worry about tomorrow,
for tomorrow will worry about itself.
Each day has enough trouble of its own.*

Matthew 6:34 NIV

*A prudent person foresees the danger ahead
and takes precautions. The simpleton goes
blindly on and suffers the consequences.*

Proverbs 27:12 NLT

*Careful planning puts you ahead in the long run;
hurry and scurry puts you further behind.*

Proverbs 21:5 MSG

There is a time for everything, and a season for every activity under heaven.

Ecclesiastes 3:1 NIV

WISDOM

Do not deceive yourselves. If any one of you thinks he is wise by the standards of this age, he should become a "fool" so that he may become wise. For the wisdom of this world is foolishness in God's sight.

1 Corinthians 3:18-19 NIV

But if any of you lacks wisdom, let him ask of God, who gives to all generously and without reproach, and it will be given to him.

James 1:5 NASB

The wisdom that is from above is first pure, then peaceable, gentle, and easy to be entreated, full of mercy and good fruits, without partiality, and without hypocrisy.

James 3:17 KJV

Reverence for the Lord is the foundation of true wisdom. The rewards of wisdom come to all who obey him.

Psalm 111:10 NLT

I will instruct you and teach you in the way you should go; I will counsel you and watch over you.

Psalm 32:8 NIV

DISCIPLINE

*No discipline seems enjoyable at the time,
but painful. Later on, however, it yields
the fruit of peace and righteousness to those
who have been trained by it.*

Hebrews 12:11 HCSB

*For this very reason, make every effort to
supplement your faith with goodness,
goodness with knowledge, knowledge with
self-control, self-control with endurance,
endurance with godliness.*

2 Peter 1:5-6 HCSB

*I discipline my body and bring it under strict
control, so that after preaching to others,
I myself will not be disqualified.*

1 Corinthians 9:27 HCSB

Therefore by their fruits you will know them.

Matthew 7:20 NKJV

The one who follows instruction is on the path to life, but the one who rejects correction goes astray.

Proverbs 10:17 HCSB

VALUES

*God's Way is not a matter of mere talk;
it's an empowered life.*

1 Corinthians 4:20 MSG

*Walk in a manner worthy of the God who
calls you into His own kingdom and glory.*

1 Thessalonians 2:12 NASB

*Therefore, since we have this ministry,
as we have received mercy, we do not give up.
Instead, we have renounced shameful secret
things, not walking in deceit or distorting
God's message, but in God's sight we commend
ourselves to every person's conscience by
an open display of the truth.*

2 Corinthians 4:1-2 HCSB

*We must not become tired of doing good.
We will receive our harvest of eternal life
at the right time if we do not give up.*

Galatians 6:9 NCV

Blessed are those who hunger and thirst for righteousness, because they will be filled.

Matthew 5:6 HCSB

WORK

Whatever your hand finds to do,
do it with all your might....

Ecclesiastes 9:10 NIV

Don't work only while being watched, in order to
please men, but as slaves of Christ, do God's will
from your heart. Render service with
a good attitude, as to the Lord and not to men.

Ephesians 6:6-7 HCSB

Do all you can to live a peaceful life.
Take care of your own business, and do your
own work as we have already told you. If you do,
then people who are not believers will respect
you, and you will not have to depend on
others for what you need.

1 Thessalonians 4:11-12 NCV

...to rejoice in his labour, this is the gift of God.

Ecclesiastes 5:19 KJV

Work hard so God can approve you. Be a good worker, one who does not need to be ashamed and who correctly explains the word of truth.

2 Timothy 2:15 NLT

ANGER

Jesus called the crowd to him and said,
"Listen and understand. What goes into
a man's mouth does not make him 'unclean,'
but what comes out of his mouth,
that is what makes him 'unclean.'"

Matthew 15:10 NIV

A person who quickly gets angry causes trouble.
But a person who controls his temper
stops a quarrel.

Proverbs 15:18 ICB

My dear brothers and sisters, be quick to listen,
slow to speak, and slow to get angry. Your anger
can never make things right in God's sight.

James 1:19-20 NLT

Foolish people lose their tempers,
but wise people control theirs.

Proverbs 29:11 NCV

Bad temper is contagious— don't get infected.

Proverbs 22:25 MSG

JESUS

Then Jesus spoke to them again:
"I am the light of the world. Anyone who
follows Me will never walk in the darkness,
but will have the light of life."

John 8:12 HCSB

At the name of Jesus every knee should bow,
of those in heaven, and of those on earth,
and of those under the earth, and that every
tongue should confess that Jesus Christ is Lord,
to the glory of God the Father.

Philippians 2:10-11 NKJV

Jesus answered, "I am the way and the truth
and the life. No one comes to the Father
except through me."

John 14:6 NIV

Jesus Christ is the same yesterday
and today and forever.

Hebrews 13:8 NASB

I am the door. If anyone enters by Me, he will be saved.

John 10:9 NKJV